TOONED IN

To Jeani, Maggie and Alex

Published by The Cincinnati Post
125 E. Court St.
Cincinnati, Ohio 45202

Special thanks to WVXU and the Merton Press

Library of Congress Cataloging Data:
Stahler, Jeff.
Tooned In: A Collection of Editorial Cartoons by Jeff Stahler.
"Library of Congress Catalog Card Number:" 94-67858

ISBN: 0-933002-07-6

I dread passing the receptionist's desk on the 19th floor here at the Enquirer Building. Nothing personal, Nancy. It's just that every morning around eleven a big stack of that day's Cincinnati Posts is deposited there for our staff.

Now, eleven o'clock is a vulnerable time of the day for me. I've usually digested the news and am rummaging through the crude sketches on my desk to see if any look promising enough to invest some ink and a good sheet of paper in. Usually the muses turn me down, and I wander around the newsroom awhile trailing a little black cloud and the fear that maybe this is The Day When Nothing Will Come.

This is when I come across the stack of Posts. And Jeff Stahler's cartoon.

Chances are he's leapt upon some issue that is only beginning to dimly dawn upon me as a topic. And with deceptively few lines nailed it to the wall. Cleverly. Humorously. And with it, my now-limp ego.

Bobbitted again.

And here's the part I don't know how he

pulls off. Invariably a colleague will then pass me, peer over my shoulder at the cartoon, laugh and say, "Hey, did you see he made Newsweek this week?"

Again? Ooch, that hurts.

The maddening thing is Jeff's a great guy, too. It'd be really convenient to loathe him, but I can't. He coaches his kids' soccer teams. His wife's a music teacher, for gawdsake. He's genuinely likable. Hell, even Tom Luken treats him courteously.

It gets mighty hot in these trenches, let me tell you, but I think Jeff and I both enjoy our friendly rivalry. We have a different bent on things, so it's easy to enjoy each other's work. And Lord knows we have enough bogus public figures in this town to go around. Why, one Marge Schott can feed a half-dozen hungry cartoonists, easy.

So have fun with this fabulous book. But, listen, do me a favor. the next time you're tempted to tell me about the latest great Stahler cartoon, just keep it to yourself, OK?

Believe me, I've already seen it.

I'm not really sure how I first met Jeff Stahler...I know it was at least nine or ten years ago and somehow we talked him into appearing on the air during Scott Simon's Weekend Edition as a guest. At the time I didn't really know how much Jeff enjoyed WVXU and Scott Simon, in particular. For many years I'd laughed at, cried over, and occasionally uttered a few "blue words" at Jeff's work and this is probably the highest compliment anyone can pay to an editorial cartoonist.

Compared to some of us who more closely resemble fossils than breathing human beings, Jeff is a youngster (or at least he was when I first met him). Despite his age at the time, however, it was patently clear to me that this guy was going places. For years, on the air with Jeff, I watched him scribble out cartoons on the fly as listeners would call in. I stared at this guy with so much obvious talent and wondered why he got so much and I had so little but then I remembered a line worth living by: "Life isn't always fair!"

Jeff has, above all else, forced those of us who enjoy his work to think. In the hustle of making a daily buck, we frequently don't have time (or make time) to think. What Jeff Stahler offers us is a precious commodity of incalculable value and I'm proud to count myself among his fans and his friends.

A few months ago we were talking with Jeff about his work and why he hadn't yet published a book of his best cartoons. He noted that he, too, was interested in such a venture. Before long, a few creative juices began heating up and within a few hours we hammered out the basis of a fun cooperative business venture. WVXU agreed to help produce the book and, in return, a special edition was created for the station to use for its members. The WVXU Special Edition of "Tooned In" even has a few special, first-ever cartoons reflecting Jeff's slightly off-beat perceptions of radio.

This has been a particularly satisfying experience for all of us at the WVXU stations. It's a pure delight to work with someone of Jeff's caliber and genius. He is clearly one of America's top editorial cartoonists who is now read in scores of newspapers and magazines all over the nation. We're proud of this book and Jeff's dedication to all that WVXU and public radio stand for. Thanks, Jeff, for the chance to say a few words. Now...read on and have a delightful time! I did.

Dr. Jim King
Director of Radio
The VXU Network

STAHLER
©THE CINCINNATI POST. 1992.

HILLARY

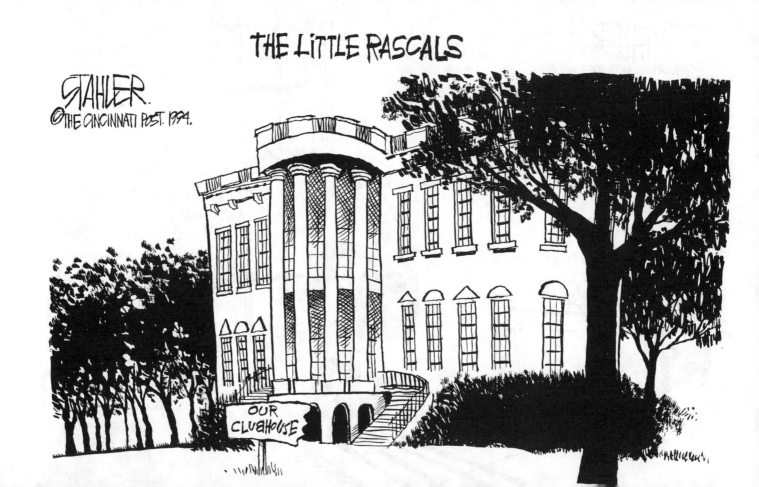

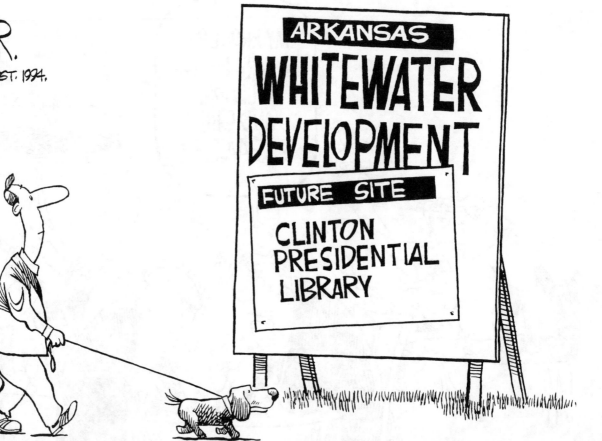

ARKANSAS

WHITEWATER DEVELOPMENT

FUTURE SITE

CLINTON PRESIDENTIAL LIBRARY

STAHLER.
©THE CINCINNATI POST·1990

BOOM BOOM BOOM BOOM BOOM BOOM
BOOM BOOM BOOM BOOM BOOM BOOM

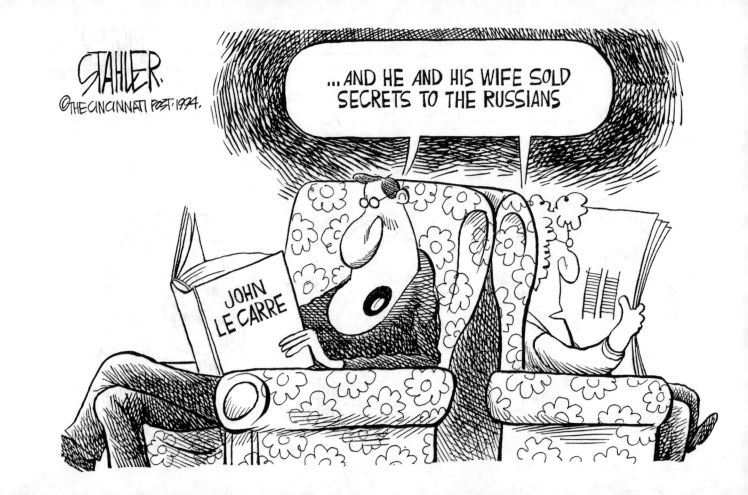

THE AMERICAN SPORTSMAN...

STAHLER.
©THE CINCINNATI POST.
1994.

NRA

STAHLER.
©THE CINCINNATI POST. 1993.

"WHAT A GREAT PLACE FOR A THEME PARK!"

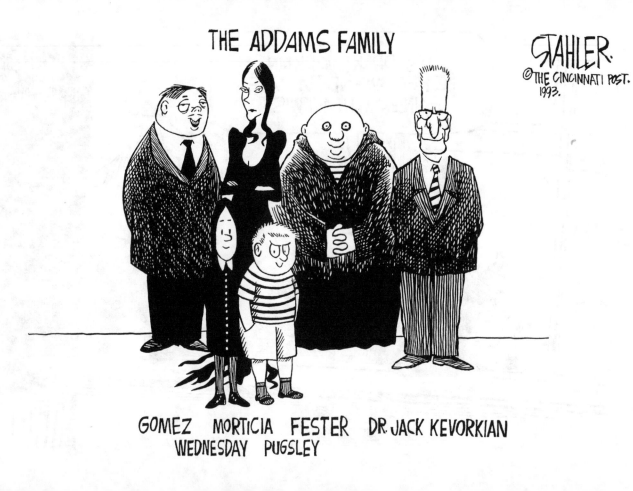

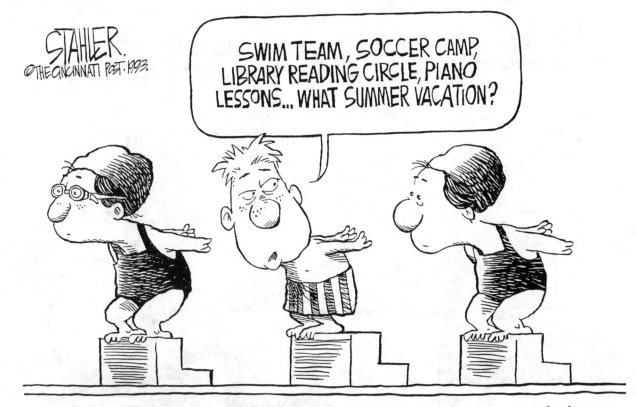

EVOLUTION OF A CAREER...

TONYA HARDING PREPARES FOR THE OLYMPICS...

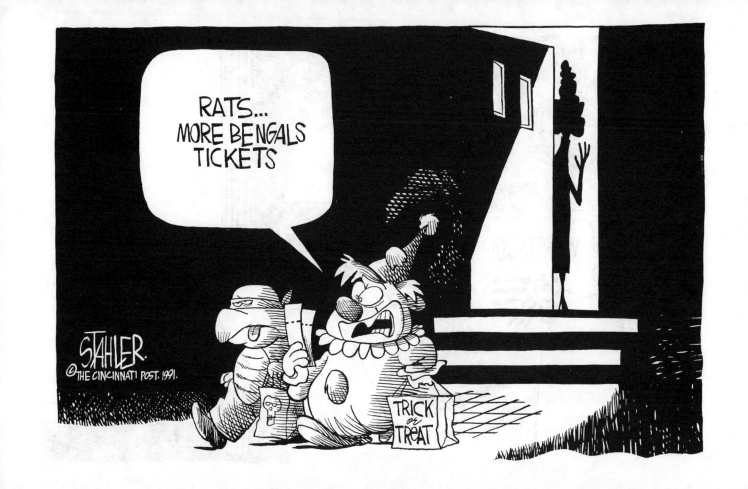

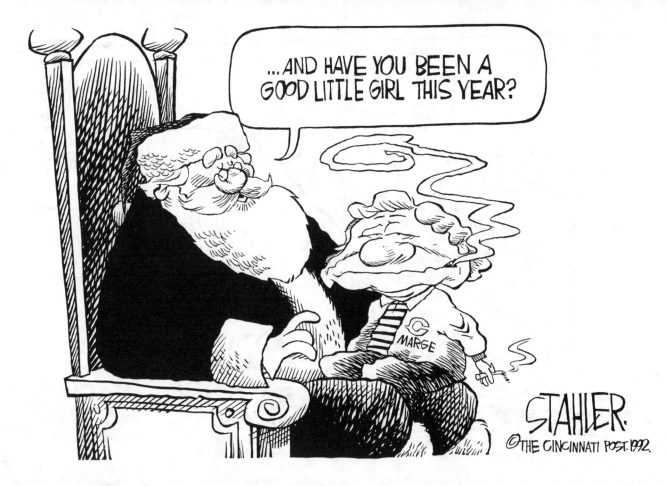

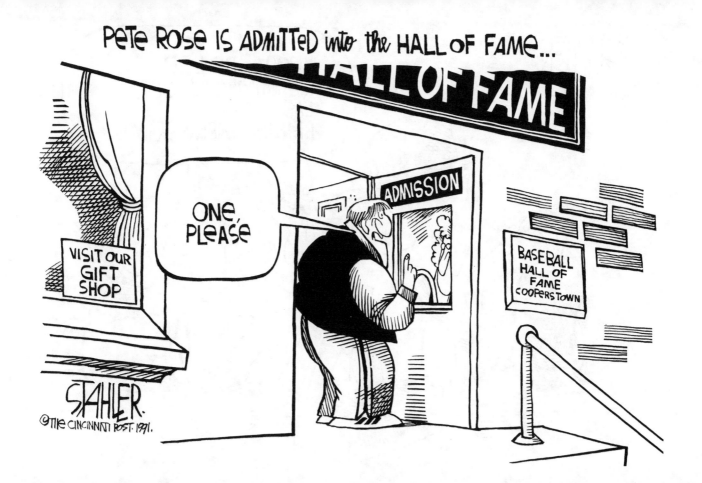